# 50 Gut Health Recipes for Home

By: Kelly Johnson

# Table of Contents

- Gut-Healing Bone Broth
- Kimchi Fried Rice
- Gut-Healthy Green Smoothie
- Roasted Vegetable Quinoa Bowl
- Turmeric Ginger Tea
- Lemon Garlic Salmon
- Gut-Friendly Chicken Soup
- Fermented Vegetables
- Coconut Yogurt Parfait
- Miso Soup with Tofu and Wakame
- Gut-Healing Vegetable Stir-Fry
- Tempeh Tacos with Avocado Crema
- Gut-Healthy Overnight Oats
- Gut-Healing Chicken Bone Broth Soup
- Sourdough Bread
- Gut-Friendly Lentil Salad
- Kombucha
- Gut-Healing Beef Stew
- Probiotic-Rich Sauerkraut
- Gut-Healthy Chia Pudding
- Gut-Healing Turkey and Rice Congee
- Gut-Friendly Zucchini Noodles with Pesto
- Fermented Pickles
- Gut-Healing Coconut Curry
- Gut-Friendly Banana Smoothie Bowl
- Kimchi Pancakes
- Gut-Healthy Quinoa Salad
- Gut-Healing Chicken and Rice Soup
- Gut-Friendly Sourdough Pancakes
- Fermented Beet Kvass
- Gut-Healing Sweet Potato and Lentil Curry
- Gut-Friendly Overnight Chia Seed Pudding
- Gut-Healthy Roasted Brussels Sprouts
- Gut-Healing Turmeric Golden Milk
- Fermented Carrots

- Gut-Friendly Coconut Kefir
- Gut-Healing Vegetable Broth
- Gut-Friendly Chickpea Salad
- Gut-Healthy Roasted Cauliflower
- Fermented Cabbage Kimchi
- Gut-Healing Ginger Tea
- Gut-Friendly Spaghetti Squash with Marinara Sauce
- Gut-Healthy Almond Butter Smoothie
- Fermented Garlic Dill Pickles
- Gut-Healing Chicken and Vegetable Stir-Fry
- Gut-Friendly Buckwheat Pancakes
- Gut-Healthy Roasted Beet Salad
- Fermented Jalapeno Hot Sauce
- Gut-Healing Turmeric Chicken Soup
- Gut-Friendly Coconut Flour Banana Bread

Gut-Healing Bone Broth

Ingredients:

- 2-3 pounds of mixed bones (such as chicken, beef, or pork bones)
- 2 carrots, chopped
- 2 celery stalks, chopped
- 1 onion, chopped
- 4 cloves garlic, smashed
- 2 tablespoons apple cider vinegar
- 1 tablespoon whole peppercorns
- 2 bay leaves
- Water, enough to cover the bones
- Optional: 1 tablespoon turmeric powder, 1-inch piece of ginger, sliced

Instructions:

1. Preheat your oven to 400°F (200°C). Place the bones on a baking sheet and roast them in the oven for about 30 minutes, or until they are browned.
2. Transfer the roasted bones to a large stockpot or slow cooker. Add the chopped carrots, celery, onion, garlic, apple cider vinegar, peppercorns, and bay leaves to the pot.
3. If using, add the turmeric powder and sliced ginger for additional gut-healing benefits.
4. Fill the pot with enough water to cover the bones and vegetables completely.
5. Bring the mixture to a boil over high heat. Once boiling, reduce the heat to low and let the broth simmer gently. If using a stockpot, partially cover with a lid. If using a slow cooker, cover with the lid.
6. Let the broth simmer for at least 8 hours, or up to 24 hours, to extract all the nutrients from the bones and vegetables. Skim off any foam or impurities that rise to the surface during cooking.
7. Once the broth is done simmering, remove the bones and vegetables with a slotted spoon or strainer. Discard the solids.
8. Strain the broth through a fine mesh strainer or cheesecloth to remove any remaining particles.
9. Let the broth cool slightly before transferring it to containers for storage. Store the bone broth in the refrigerator for up to 5 days, or freeze it for longer storage.

10. Enjoy the gut-healing bone broth on its own, or use it as a base for soups, stews, sauces, and other dishes. It's a nutritious and comforting addition to any diet, especially for promoting gut health!

**Kimchi Fried Rice**

Ingredients:

- 2 cups cooked rice (preferably day-old)
- 1 cup kimchi, chopped
- 2 tablespoons kimchi juice
- 2 tablespoons vegetable oil
- 2 cloves garlic, minced
- 1 small onion, finely chopped
- 1 carrot, diced
- 1 cup frozen peas, thawed
- 2 green onions, chopped
- 2 tablespoons soy sauce
- 1 tablespoon sesame oil
- 1 teaspoon sugar (optional)
- 2 eggs, beaten (optional)
- Sesame seeds, for garnish (optional)

Instructions:

1. Heat 1 tablespoon of vegetable oil in a large skillet or wok over medium-high heat.
2. Add the minced garlic and chopped onion to the skillet. Stir-fry for 2-3 minutes, or until the onion is translucent and fragrant.
3. Add the chopped kimchi and diced carrot to the skillet. Stir-fry for another 2-3 minutes, or until the carrot is slightly softened.
4. Push the vegetables to one side of the skillet and add the remaining tablespoon of vegetable oil to the empty side.
5. Add the cooked rice to the skillet, breaking up any clumps with a spatula. Stir-fry the rice with the vegetables for 3-4 minutes, or until heated through.
6. In a small bowl, mix together the kimchi juice, soy sauce, sesame oil, and sugar (if using). Pour the sauce over the fried rice and toss to combine.
7. Add the thawed peas and chopped green onions to the skillet. Stir-fry for another 1-2 minutes, or until the peas are heated through.

8. If using, push the fried rice to one side of the skillet and pour the beaten eggs into the empty side. Cook the eggs, stirring occasionally, until scrambled and cooked through.
9. Once the eggs are cooked, stir them into the fried rice until evenly distributed.
10. Remove the skillet from the heat and transfer the kimchi fried rice to serving plates.
11. Garnish with sesame seeds, if desired, and serve hot.

Enjoy this flavorful and satisfying Kimchi Fried Rice as a delicious meal or side dish!

**Gut-Healthy Green Smoothie**

Ingredients:

- 1 cup spinach leaves, tightly packed
- 1/2 cup kale leaves, stems removed
- 1/2 cup cucumber, chopped
- 1/2 cup celery, chopped
- 1/2 cup frozen pineapple chunks
- 1/2 cup frozen mango chunks
- 1 banana, fresh or frozen
- 1 tablespoon chia seeds
- 1 cup coconut water or filtered water
- Juice of 1/2 lemon or lime
- Optional: 1 tablespoon fresh ginger, grated

Instructions:

1. Place all the ingredients in a blender in the order listed.
2. Blend on high speed until smooth and creamy, adding more coconut water or water as needed to reach your desired consistency.
3. Taste the smoothie and adjust the flavor, if desired, by adding more lemon or lime juice for acidity or more banana or pineapple for sweetness.
4. Pour the smoothie into glasses and serve immediately.
5. Enjoy this refreshing and nutrient-packed Gut-Healthy Green Smoothie as a nutritious breakfast or snack to support your gut health!

**Roasted Vegetable Quinoa Bowl**

Ingredients:

For the roasted vegetables:

- 2 cups mixed vegetables (such as bell peppers, zucchini, carrots, cherry tomatoes, broccoli florets)
- 2 tablespoons olive oil
- 1 teaspoon garlic powder
- 1 teaspoon dried herbs (such as thyme, rosemary, or oregano)
- Salt and black pepper to taste

For the quinoa:

- 1 cup quinoa, rinsed
- 2 cups water or vegetable broth
- Salt to taste

For the dressing:

- 2 tablespoons olive oil
- 1 tablespoon balsamic vinegar
- 1 teaspoon Dijon mustard
- 1 clove garlic, minced
- Salt and black pepper to taste

Optional toppings:

- Avocado slices
- Fresh herbs (such as parsley or basil)
- Toasted nuts or seeds (such as almonds, pumpkin seeds, or sunflower seeds)
- Crumbled feta or goat cheese

Instructions:

1. Preheat your oven to 400°F (200°C). Line a baking sheet with parchment paper or aluminum foil for easy cleanup.
2. In a large mixing bowl, toss the mixed vegetables with olive oil, garlic powder, dried herbs, salt, and black pepper until evenly coated.
3. Spread the seasoned vegetables in a single layer on the prepared baking sheet.
4. Roast the vegetables in the preheated oven for 20-25 minutes, or until they are tender and slightly caramelized, stirring halfway through cooking.
5. While the vegetables are roasting, prepare the quinoa. In a medium saucepan, combine the rinsed quinoa and water or vegetable broth. Bring to a boil over high heat.
6. Reduce the heat to low, cover, and simmer for 15-20 minutes, or until the quinoa is cooked and the liquid is absorbed. Remove from heat and let it sit, covered, for 5 minutes. Fluff the quinoa with a fork.
7. In a small bowl, whisk together the olive oil, balsamic vinegar, Dijon mustard, minced garlic, salt, and black pepper to make the dressing.
8. To assemble the quinoa bowls, divide the cooked quinoa among serving bowls. Top with the roasted vegetables.
9. Drizzle the dressing over the quinoa and vegetables.
10. Add any optional toppings, such as avocado slices, fresh herbs, toasted nuts or seeds, and crumbled cheese.
11. Serve the Roasted Vegetable Quinoa Bowls warm, and enjoy this nutritious and flavorful meal!

**Turmeric Ginger Tea**

Ingredients:

- 2 cups water
- 1-inch piece of fresh ginger, sliced
- 1 teaspoon ground turmeric or 1-inch piece of fresh turmeric, sliced
- 1 teaspoon honey or maple syrup (optional)
- Juice of 1/2 lemon (optional)
- Pinch of black pepper (optional)

Instructions:

1. In a small saucepan, bring the water to a boil.
2. Add the sliced ginger and turmeric to the boiling water.
3. Reduce the heat to low and let the mixture simmer for 5-10 minutes to infuse the flavors.
4. Remove the saucepan from the heat and strain the tea to remove the ginger and turmeric pieces.
5. Stir in honey or maple syrup, if using, to sweeten the tea to your taste.
6. Optionally, add a squeeze of lemon juice for a citrusy flavor and a pinch of black pepper to enhance the absorption of turmeric's active compound, curcumin.
7. Pour the turmeric ginger tea into mugs and serve it hot.
8. Enjoy this soothing and warming Turmeric Ginger Tea as a comforting beverage any time of day!

**Lemon Garlic Salmon**

Ingredients:

- 4 salmon fillets (about 6 ounces each), skin-on or skinless
- Salt and black pepper, to taste
- 2 tablespoons olive oil
- 4 cloves garlic, minced
- Zest and juice of 1 lemon
- 2 tablespoons chopped fresh parsley
- Lemon slices, for garnish (optional)

Instructions:

1. Preheat your oven to 400°F (200°C). Line a baking sheet with parchment paper or aluminum foil for easy cleanup.
2. Pat the salmon fillets dry with paper towels and season them generously with salt and black pepper on both sides.
3. In a small bowl, mix together the olive oil, minced garlic, lemon zest, lemon juice, and chopped parsley to make the marinade.
4. Place the seasoned salmon fillets on the prepared baking sheet, spaced apart.
5. Spoon the lemon garlic marinade over the salmon fillets, making sure to coat them evenly.
6. Optionally, garnish each salmon fillet with a slice of lemon for extra flavor.
7. Bake the salmon in the preheated oven for 12-15 minutes, or until the salmon flakes easily with a fork and reaches your desired level of doneness. The cooking time may vary depending on the thickness of the salmon fillets.
8. Once cooked, remove the salmon from the oven and let it rest for a few minutes before serving.
9. Serve the Lemon Garlic Salmon hot, garnished with additional chopped parsley if desired.
10. Enjoy this flavorful and nutritious dish with your favorite side dishes, such as roasted vegetables, quinoa, or salad!

**Gut-Friendly Chicken Soup**

Ingredients:

- 1 tablespoon olive oil
- 1 onion, diced
- 2 carrots, diced
- 2 celery stalks, diced
- 3 cloves garlic, minced
- 8 cups chicken broth (homemade or low-sodium store-bought)
- 2 cups cooked shredded chicken breast
- 1 teaspoon dried thyme
- 1 teaspoon dried rosemary
- 1 bay leaf
- Salt and black pepper to taste
- 2 cups baby spinach leaves
- Juice of 1 lemon
- Fresh parsley, chopped, for garnish (optional)

Instructions:

1. In a large pot or Dutch oven, heat the olive oil over medium heat. Add the diced onion, carrots, and celery. Cook, stirring occasionally, for about 5 minutes, or until the vegetables are softened.
2. Add the minced garlic to the pot and cook for an additional 1-2 minutes, until fragrant.
3. Pour the chicken broth into the pot and bring the mixture to a simmer.
4. Stir in the shredded chicken breast, dried thyme, dried rosemary, bay leaf, salt, and black pepper.
5. Let the soup simmer, uncovered, for about 15-20 minutes to allow the flavors to meld together.
6. Add the baby spinach leaves to the pot and cook for an additional 2-3 minutes, or until wilted.
7. Remove the bay leaf from the soup and discard it.
8. Stir in the lemon juice to brighten the flavors of the soup.
9. Taste the soup and adjust the seasoning with more salt and pepper if needed.
10. Ladle the Gut-Friendly Chicken Soup into bowls and garnish with chopped fresh parsley, if desired.

11. Serve the soup hot and enjoy its nourishing and soothing properties!

This Gut-Friendly Chicken Soup is packed with wholesome ingredients and is gentle on the digestive system, making it perfect for supporting gut health.

**Fermented Vegetables**

Ingredients:

- Assorted vegetables of your choice (such as cabbage, carrots, radishes, bell peppers, cucumbers, etc.)
- 2-3 tablespoons sea salt or kosher salt (non-iodized)
- Filtered water
- Optional: herbs and spices (such as garlic, ginger, dill, mustard seeds, peppercorns, etc.)

Instructions:

1. Wash and prepare your vegetables by cutting them into desired shapes and sizes. You can shred, slice, or chop them as preferred.
2. In a large mixing bowl, combine the prepared vegetables with the salt. Massage the salt into the vegetables with your hands, squeezing them gently to release their juices.
3. Pack the salted vegetables tightly into clean, sterilized glass jars, leaving about an inch of space at the top.
4. Add any herbs and spices of your choice to the jars for additional flavor.
5. Pour enough filtered water over the vegetables to completely submerge them, ensuring they are fully covered. Leave about half an inch of space at the top of the jar to prevent overflow during fermentation.
6. Use a clean, sterilized weight or fermentation weight to keep the vegetables submerged under the brine. This helps prevent mold growth.
7. Seal the jars tightly with lids or fermentation lids.
8. Place the jars in a cool, dark place to ferment. The ideal temperature for fermentation is between 60°F to 75°F (15°C to 24°C). Fermentation times vary depending on the vegetables and ambient temperature, but most ferments take around 1 to 2 weeks.
9. Check the vegetables periodically during fermentation. You may notice bubbles forming, which is a sign that fermentation is occurring. You may also see a white film or scum on the surface, which is normal and can be skimmed off if desired.
10. Taste the fermented vegetables after about a week to gauge their flavor and texture. If they have reached your desired level of fermentation, transfer the jars to the refrigerator to slow down the fermentation process. Fermented vegetables can be stored in the refrigerator for several months.

11. Enjoy your homemade fermented vegetables as a flavorful and probiotic-rich addition to salads, sandwiches, Buddha bowls, or as a side dish with meals!

Note: Always use clean, sterilized equipment and jars when fermenting vegetables to prevent contamination. Adjust salt and water ratios based on personal preference and the type of vegetables used.

**Coconut Yogurt Parfait**

Ingredients:

- 1 cup coconut yogurt (store-bought or homemade)
- 1/2 cup granola (store-bought or homemade)
- 1/2 cup mixed fresh berries (such as strawberries, blueberries, raspberries)
- 2 tablespoons shredded coconut
- 1 tablespoon honey or maple syrup (optional)
- Fresh mint leaves for garnish (optional)

Instructions:

1. In a small bowl or glass, layer the ingredients to create the parfait. Start with a spoonful of coconut yogurt at the bottom of the bowl.
2. Add a layer of granola on top of the yogurt.
3. Spoon some mixed fresh berries over the granola layer.
4. Sprinkle shredded coconut on top of the berries.
5. Repeat the layers until you've used up all the ingredients or reached the desired height of the parfait.
6. Drizzle honey or maple syrup over the top of the parfait for added sweetness, if desired.
7. Garnish the parfait with fresh mint leaves for a pop of color and freshness.
8. Serve immediately and enjoy your delicious and nutritious Coconut Yogurt Parfait as a refreshing breakfast, snack, or dessert option!

Feel free to customize your parfait with additional toppings such as nuts, seeds, dried fruit, or a dollop of nut butter for extra flavor and texture.

**Miso Soup with Tofu and Wakame**

Ingredients:

- 4 cups dashi stock (you can make your own using kombu and bonito flakes or use instant dashi powder)
- 3 tablespoons miso paste (white or red, depending on your preference)
- 1/2 block tofu, diced into small cubes
- 1/4 cup dried wakame seaweed
- 2 green onions, thinly sliced (optional)
- 1 tablespoon soy sauce (optional)

Instructions:

1. If you're using dried wakame seaweed, rehydrate it by soaking it in warm water for about 5 minutes. Drain and set aside.
2. In a medium saucepan, bring the dashi stock to a gentle simmer over medium heat.
3. Add the diced tofu to the simmering dashi stock and let it cook for a few minutes until heated through.
4. Take a ladleful of the hot dashi stock and dissolve the miso paste in it, making sure there are no lumps.
5. Add the dissolved miso paste back into the saucepan with the tofu and dashi stock. Be careful not to let the soup come to a boil, as boiling miso can destroy its flavor.
6. Add the rehydrated wakame seaweed to the soup and let it simmer for another minute or two.
7. Taste the soup and adjust the seasoning by adding soy sauce if desired.
8. Serve the miso soup hot, garnished with thinly sliced green onions if you like.

Enjoy your homemade miso soup with tofu and wakame! It's a perfect dish for a cozy evening or as part of a Japanese-inspired meal.

**Gut-Healing Vegetable Stir-Fry**

Ingredients:

- 2 tablespoons olive oil or coconut oil
- 2 cloves garlic, minced
- 1-inch piece of ginger, minced
- 1 onion, thinly sliced
- 2 carrots, julienned
- 1 bell pepper, thinly sliced
- 1 cup broccoli florets
- 1 cup sliced mushrooms (such as shiitake or cremini)
- 2 cups spinach or kale, chopped
- 2 tablespoons tamari or soy sauce (or coconut aminos for a soy-free option)
- 1 tablespoon rice vinegar
- 1 tablespoon sesame oil
- 1 tablespoon honey or maple syrup (optional)
- Salt and pepper to taste
- Red pepper flakes (optional, for heat)
- Sesame seeds for garnish
- Cooked rice or quinoa, for serving

Instructions:

1. Heat the olive oil or coconut oil in a large skillet or wok over medium-high heat.
2. Add the minced garlic and ginger to the skillet and sauté for about 1 minute until fragrant.
3. Add the sliced onion to the skillet and cook for 2-3 minutes until softened.
4. Add the julienned carrots, sliced bell pepper, broccoli florets, and sliced mushrooms to the skillet. Stir-fry for 5-7 minutes until the vegetables are tender-crisp.
5. Stir in the chopped spinach or kale and cook for another 1-2 minutes until wilted.
6. In a small bowl, whisk together the tamari or soy sauce, rice vinegar, sesame oil, and honey or maple syrup (if using).
7. Pour the sauce over the stir-fried vegetables in the skillet and toss to coat evenly. Season with salt, pepper, and red pepper flakes to taste.
8. Cook for another 1-2 minutes until the sauce has thickened slightly and everything is heated through.

9. Remove from heat and garnish with sesame seeds.
10. Serve the gut-healing vegetable stir-fry hot over cooked rice or quinoa.

This stir-fry is not only tasty but also packed with fiber, vitamins, and antioxidants that can support your gut health. Feel free to customize it with your favorite vegetables or protein sources like tofu, tempeh, or cooked chicken. Enjoy!

**Tempeh Tacos with Avocado Crema**

Ingredients:

- 8 oz (about 225g) tempeh, crumbled or diced
- 2 tablespoons olive oil
- 1 small onion, diced
- 2 cloves garlic, minced
- 1 tablespoon chili powder
- 1 teaspoon ground cumin
- 1/2 teaspoon smoked paprika
- Salt and pepper to taste
- 1/4 cup vegetable broth or water
- Juice of 1 lime

Instructions:

1. Heat the olive oil in a skillet over medium heat. Add the diced onion and minced garlic and sauté until softened, about 2-3 minutes.
2. Add the crumbled or diced tempeh to the skillet and cook for 5-7 minutes, stirring occasionally, until it starts to brown.
3. Stir in the chili powder, cumin, smoked paprika, salt, and pepper, and cook for another 1-2 minutes to toast the spices.
4. Pour in the vegetable broth or water and lime juice, and stir to combine. Cook for an additional 3-5 minutes until the liquid has mostly evaporated and the tempeh is coated in the spices. Remove from heat.

Avocado Crema:

Ingredients:

- 1 ripe avocado
- 1/4 cup plain Greek yogurt or dairy-free yogurt
- Juice of 1 lime
- 1 tablespoon chopped cilantro
- Salt and pepper to taste

Instructions:

1. Scoop the flesh of the avocado into a blender or food processor.
2. Add the Greek yogurt, lime juice, chopped cilantro, salt, and pepper.
3. Blend until smooth and creamy. If the crema is too thick, you can add a little water to thin it out.

Assembling the Tacos:

Additional Ingredients:

- 8 small corn or flour tortillas, warmed
- Shredded lettuce
- Diced tomatoes
- Sliced radishes
- Chopped cilantro
- Lime wedges

Instructions:

1. Fill each tortilla with a generous spoonful of the tempeh taco filling.
2. Top with shredded lettuce, diced tomatoes, sliced radishes, and chopped cilantro.
3. Drizzle with avocado crema and serve with lime wedges on the side.

Enjoy your delicious tempeh tacos with avocado crema! They're perfect for a quick and flavorful plant-based meal.

**Gut-Healthy Overnight Oats**

Ingredients:

- 1/2 cup rolled oats (gluten-free if needed)
- 1 tablespoon chia seeds
- 1 tablespoon ground flaxseeds
- 1/2 cup yogurt (Greek yogurt or dairy-free yogurt for a vegan option)
- 1/2 cup milk (dairy or plant-based)
- 1/2 teaspoon ground cinnamon
- 1/2 teaspoon pure vanilla extract
- 1 tablespoon honey or maple syrup (optional)
- 1/2 cup mixed berries (such as blueberries, raspberries, or strawberries)
- 1 ripe banana, sliced
- Additional toppings of your choice (such as nuts, seeds, or coconut flakes)

Instructions:

1. In a mason jar or airtight container, combine the rolled oats, chia seeds, ground flaxseeds, yogurt, milk, cinnamon, vanilla extract, and honey or maple syrup (if using). Stir until well combined.
2. Add the mixed berries and sliced banana to the mixture, stirring gently to distribute them evenly.
3. Cover the jar or container with a lid and refrigerate overnight, or for at least 4 hours, to allow the oats to soften and the flavors to meld.
4. In the morning, give the overnight oats a good stir. If the consistency is too thick for your liking, you can add a splash of milk to loosen it up.
5. Serve the gut-healthy overnight oats cold, straight from the refrigerator, or warm them up in the microwave if you prefer.
6. Before serving, top the oats with additional toppings of your choice, such as nuts, seeds, or coconut flakes, for added texture and flavor.

Why These Ingredients are Gut-Healthy:

- Oats: Rich in soluble fiber, oats help regulate bowel movements and support a healthy digestive system.
- Chia Seeds: Packed with fiber and omega-3 fatty acids, chia seeds promote gut health by supporting regularity and reducing inflammation.

- Flaxseeds: Another excellent source of fiber and omega-3 fatty acids, flaxseeds contribute to healthy digestion and may reduce the risk of certain digestive disorders.
- Yogurt: Contains probiotics, beneficial bacteria that promote a healthy balance of gut flora and support digestive health.
- Berries: High in antioxidants and fiber, berries help nourish the gut microbiota and support overall digestive function.
- Banana: Contains prebiotic fiber, which serves as fuel for the beneficial bacteria in your gut, promoting a healthy balance of gut flora.

Enjoy your gut-healthy overnight oats as a nutritious and delicious breakfast option!

**Gut-Healing Chicken Bone Broth Soup**

Ingredients:

For the broth:

- 1 whole organic chicken
- 4-6 chicken feet (optional, but adds extra gelatin and collagen)
- 4-6 quarts of water
- 2 tablespoons apple cider vinegar
- 2 onions, peeled and quartered
- 3 carrots, chopped
- 3 celery stalks, chopped
- 4 cloves garlic, smashed
- 1 tablespoon whole black peppercorns
- 2 bay leaves
- Handful of fresh parsley

For the soup:

- 2 tablespoons olive oil
- 1 onion, finely chopped
- 2 carrots, diced
- 2 celery stalks, diced
- 3 cloves garlic, minced
- 1 teaspoon ground turmeric
- Salt and pepper to taste
- 4 cups chopped spinach or kale
- Cooked shredded chicken from the broth
- Fresh lemon juice (optional, for serving)
- Fresh parsley, chopped (for garnish)

Instructions:

1. In a large stockpot, combine the whole chicken, chicken feet (if using), water, apple cider vinegar, onions, carrots, celery, garlic, peppercorns, bay leaves, and

parsley. Bring to a boil, then reduce the heat to low and let simmer for 4-6 hours, skimming off any foam that rises to the top.
2. Once the broth is done simmering, strain it through a fine-mesh sieve into another large pot or bowl. Discard the solids and set the broth aside. You can also pick off any remaining chicken meat from the bones to use in the soup.
3. In a separate large pot, heat the olive oil over medium heat. Add the chopped onion, carrots, and celery, and cook until softened, about 5 minutes. Add the minced garlic and ground turmeric, and cook for another minute until fragrant.
4. Pour the strained broth into the pot with the sautéed vegetables. Bring to a simmer and cook for another 10-15 minutes to allow the flavors to meld.
5. Add the chopped spinach or kale and shredded chicken to the soup, and cook for another 5 minutes until the greens are wilted and the chicken is heated through. Season with salt and pepper to taste.
6. Ladle the soup into bowls and squeeze a bit of fresh lemon juice over each serving if desired. Garnish with chopped fresh parsley and serve hot.

Enjoy your gut-healing chicken bone broth soup!

**Sourdough Bread**

Ingredients:

- 1 cup active sourdough starter
- 1 1/2 cups lukewarm water
- 4 cups bread flour or all-purpose flour
- 1 1/2 teaspoons salt

Instructions:

Day 1: Prepare the Starter

1. If your sourdough starter has been refrigerated, take it out and let it come to room temperature.
2. In a large mixing bowl, combine 1 cup of the active sourdough starter with 1 1/2 cups lukewarm water.
3. Add 4 cups of bread flour or all-purpose flour to the bowl and mix until a shaggy dough forms.
4. Cover the bowl loosely with plastic wrap or a kitchen towel and let it sit at room temperature for about 4-6 hours, or until it's visibly bubbly and has doubled in size. This is called the "bulk fermentation" stage.

Day 1 (later): Mixing and Shaping

5. After the bulk fermentation, add 1 1/2 teaspoons of salt to the dough.

6. Use your hands or a dough scraper to fold and incorporate the salt into the dough.
7. Cover the bowl again and let the dough rest for another 30 minutes to 1 hour.

Day 1 (later): Folding

8. Perform a series of "stretch and fold" techniques every 30 minutes for the next 2-3 hours. To do this, wet your hands slightly, grab one edge of the dough, stretch it upwards, and fold it over the center. Repeat this process from all four sides of the dough.

9. After the last fold, cover the dough and let it rest for another 1-2 hours, or until it has increased in volume by about 20-30%.

Day 1 (later): Pre-shaping

10. Flour a clean work surface and gently turn the dough out onto it.

11. Using a bench scraper, divide the dough in half if making two loaves or leave it as one if making a single large loaf.
12. Gently shape each portion into a round by folding the edges towards the center, creating tension on the surface. Let them rest for 20-30 minutes, covered with a kitchen towel or plastic wrap.

Day 1 (later): Final Shaping and Proofing

13. Shape the dough into its final shape. For a round loaf, gently flip the dough over and pull the edges towards the center, creating tension on the surface. Place the shaped dough onto a well-floured proofing basket or a bowl lined with a kitchen towel, seam side up.

14. Cover the dough and let it proof at room temperature for 2-4 hours, or until it has visibly expanded and feels airy when gently pressed with a finger. Alternatively, you can retard the proofing process by placing the dough in the refrigerator overnight (8-12 hours) for enhanced flavor development.

Day 2: Baking

15. About 30 minutes before baking, preheat your oven to 450°F (230°C). Place a Dutch oven or a baking stone on the center rack to preheat as well.

16. Once the oven is preheated, carefully transfer the proofed dough to the hot Dutch oven or baking stone. Score the top of the dough with a sharp knife or razor blade to allow for expansion.
17. Cover the Dutch oven with its lid or place a large oven-safe bowl over the dough to create steam. Bake covered for 20-25 minutes.
18. Remove the lid or bowl and continue baking for another 20-25 minutes, or until the crust is deeply golden brown and the bread sounds hollow when tapped on the bottom.
19. Transfer the bread to a wire rack and let it cool completely before slicing.

Enjoy your homemade sourdough bread!

**Gut-Friendly Lentil Salad**

Ingredients:

- 1 cup dried lentils (green or brown), rinsed and drained
- 2 1/2 cups water or vegetable broth
- 1/2 teaspoon salt
- 1/2 cup cherry tomatoes, halved
- 1/2 cucumber, diced
- 1/4 cup red onion, finely chopped
- 1/4 cup fresh parsley, chopped
- 2 tablespoons extra virgin olive oil
- 2 tablespoons apple cider vinegar or lemon juice
- 1 clove garlic, minced
- Salt and pepper to taste
- Optional add-ins: diced bell peppers, shredded carrots, chopped spinach, feta cheese, avocado

Instructions:

1. In a medium saucepan, combine the rinsed lentils, water or vegetable broth, and salt. Bring to a boil over high heat.
2. Reduce the heat to low, cover, and simmer for 20-25 minutes, or until the lentils are tender but still hold their shape. Drain any excess liquid and let the lentils cool to room temperature.
3. In a large mixing bowl, combine the cooked lentils, cherry tomatoes, cucumber, red onion, and fresh parsley.
4. In a small bowl, whisk together the extra virgin olive oil, apple cider vinegar or lemon juice, minced garlic, salt, and pepper to make the dressing.
5. Pour the dressing over the lentil mixture and toss gently to combine, ensuring all ingredients are evenly coated.
6. Taste and adjust the seasoning if needed. You can add more salt, pepper, or vinegar to suit your taste preferences.
7. If desired, add any optional add-ins such as diced bell peppers, shredded carrots, chopped spinach, feta cheese, or avocado.
8. Serve the lentil salad immediately at room temperature, or chill it in the refrigerator for at least 30 minutes to allow the flavors to meld before serving.

This gut-friendly lentil salad is packed with fiber, protein, and healthy fats, making it a satisfying and nutritious meal or side dish. Enjoy!

## Kombucha

Ingredients:

- 1 SCOBY (you can purchase one online or get one from a friend)
- 1 cup starter tea (liquid from a previous batch of kombucha or store-bought raw, unflavored kombucha)
- 4-6 black or green tea bags (avoid flavored teas)
- 1 cup granulated sugar
- Water
- Optional flavorings: fruit juice, sliced fruit, herbs, spices, etc.

Equipment:

- Large glass jar or brewing vessel (at least 1-gallon capacity)
- Clean cloth or paper towel
- Rubber band or string
- Bottles for bottling (glass bottles with flip-top lids work well)

Instructions:

1. Boil 4 cups of water in a pot. Once boiling, remove from heat and add the tea bags. Let the tea steep for about 5-10 minutes, then remove the tea bags.
2. Stir in the sugar until completely dissolved. This sweetened tea mixture is called the "sweet tea."
3. Allow the sweet tea to cool to room temperature. Do not add the SCOBY to hot tea, as it can damage the culture.
4. Once the sweet tea has cooled, transfer it to your brewing vessel. Add enough water to fill the vessel, leaving some space at the top.
5. Carefully add the SCOBY and the starter tea to the vessel.
6. Cover the vessel with a clean cloth or paper towel and secure it with a rubber band or string. This will prevent dust and insects from getting into the kombucha while allowing airflow.
7. Place the vessel in a warm, dark place (ideally between 70-80°F or 21-27°C) to ferment. Avoid direct sunlight, as it can harm the SCOBY.

8. Let the kombucha ferment for 7-14 days, depending on your taste preferences. The longer it ferments, the more acidic it will become.
9. After the fermentation period, taste the kombucha. If it's too sweet, let it ferment for a few more days. If it's too sour, it's ready to bottle.
10. Once you're happy with the flavor, carefully remove the SCOBY from the kombucha using clean hands or utensils.
11. If desired, you can flavor the kombucha by adding fruit juice, sliced fruit, herbs, spices, etc., to the bottles before bottling.
12. Transfer the kombucha to clean bottles, leaving some space at the top. Seal the bottles tightly.
13. Let the bottled kombucha sit at room temperature for 1-3 days for secondary fermentation. This will create natural carbonation.
14. After secondary fermentation, refrigerate the bottles to slow down the fermentation process and chill the kombucha.
15. Enjoy your homemade kombucha straight from the fridge!

Remember to always use clean utensils and containers when brewing kombucha to prevent contamination. Additionally, be cautious when handling the SCOBY to avoid introducing harmful bacteria. With practice, you'll become more familiar with the fermentation process and can adjust the recipe to suit your taste preferences.

**Gut-Healing Beef Stew**

Ingredients:

- 1 pound grass-fed beef stew meat, cut into bite-sized pieces
- 2 tablespoons olive oil or coconut oil
- 4 cups low-sodium beef broth
- 2 cups water
- 2 medium carrots, chopped
- 2 celery stalks, chopped
- 1 large potato, peeled and diced (optional, omit if sensitive to nightshades)
- 1 parsnip, peeled and chopped
- 1/2 cup chopped leeks or onions
- 2 cloves garlic, minced
- 1 teaspoon dried thyme
- 1 teaspoon dried rosemary
- 1 bay leaf
- Salt and pepper to taste
- Chopped fresh parsley for garnish (optional)

Instructions:

1. In a large pot or Dutch oven, heat the olive oil over medium heat. Add the beef stew meat and brown on all sides, about 5 minutes. Remove the beef from the pot and set aside.
2. In the same pot, add the chopped leeks or onions and sauté until softened, about 3-4 minutes. Add the minced garlic and sauté for another minute until fragrant.
3. Return the browned beef to the pot. Add the carrots, celery, parsnip, and potato (if using) to the pot.
4. Pour in the beef broth and water, making sure the vegetables and meat are covered with liquid. Add the dried thyme, dried rosemary, bay leaf, and season with salt and pepper to taste.
5. Bring the stew to a boil, then reduce the heat to low. Cover and simmer for 1 1/2 to 2 hours, or until the beef is tender and the vegetables are cooked through.
6. Once the stew is done cooking, taste and adjust the seasoning if needed. Remove the bay leaf before serving.

7. Ladle the beef stew into bowls and garnish with chopped fresh parsley, if desired. Serve hot and enjoy!

This gut-healing beef stew is rich in flavor and nutrients, making it a comforting meal for anyone looking to support their digestive health. Feel free to customize the recipe by adding other gut-friendly ingredients like mushrooms, bone broth, or leafy greens.

**Probiotic-Rich Sauerkraut**

Ingredients:

- 1 medium-sized head of cabbage (green or purple)
- 1 tablespoon sea salt or kosher salt (avoid iodized salt)
- Optional: Caraway seeds, juniper berries, garlic cloves, shredded carrots, shredded beets, or other flavorings

Equipment:

- Large mixing bowl
- Knife or mandoline slicer
- Clean quart-sized mason jar or fermentation crock
- Small weight (such as a clean rock or fermentation weight)
- Clean cloth or paper towel
- Rubber band or string

Instructions:

1. Remove any outer leaves from the cabbage and reserve one or two large leaves. These will be used later to keep the shredded cabbage submerged in brine.
2. Cut the cabbage into quarters and remove the core. Slice the cabbage thinly using a knife or mandoline slicer. Place the shredded cabbage in a large mixing bowl.
3. Sprinkle the salt over the shredded cabbage. Massage the cabbage with your hands for a few minutes until it starts to release its juices. This process helps to break down the cell walls of the cabbage and create a brine.
4. If using any additional flavorings like caraway seeds, juniper berries, garlic cloves, shredded carrots, or beets, add them to the bowl and mix well with the cabbage.
5. Pack the cabbage mixture tightly into a clean quart-sized mason jar or fermentation crock, pressing down firmly with your hands or a clean utensil to remove any air pockets. Leave about 2 inches of space at the top of the jar.
6. Pour any remaining liquid from the mixing bowl into the jar to cover the cabbage completely. The cabbage should be submerged in brine to prevent mold growth.

7. Take the reserved cabbage leaves and place them on top of the shredded cabbage in the jar to create a barrier between the cabbage and the air.
8. Place a small weight on top of the cabbage leaves to keep everything submerged under the brine. This can be a clean rock, fermentation weight, or a smaller jar filled with water.
9. Cover the jar with a clean cloth or paper towel and secure it with a rubber band or string. This allows airflow while keeping out dust and insects.
10. Place the jar in a cool, dark place to ferment. Check the sauerkraut every day or two to ensure that the cabbage remains submerged under the brine. If necessary, press down on the weight to release any trapped air bubbles.
11. Ferment the sauerkraut for 1-4 weeks, depending on your taste preferences. The longer it ferments, the tangier and more probiotic-rich it will become.
12. Once the sauerkraut reaches your desired level of fermentation, remove the weight and cabbage leaves from the top of the jar. Tightly seal the jar with a lid and transfer it to the refrigerator to slow down the fermentation process.
13. Enjoy your homemade probiotic-rich sauerkraut as a tasty condiment or side dish! It pairs well with sandwiches, salads, sausages, and more.

**Gut-Healthy Chia Pudding**

Ingredients:

- 1/4 cup chia seeds
- 1 cup unsweetened almond milk, coconut milk, or any other milk of your choice
- 1-2 tablespoons maple syrup, honey, or other sweetener of your choice (optional)
- 1/2 teaspoon vanilla extract
- Optional toppings: fresh fruit (e.g., berries, banana slices), nuts, seeds, shredded coconut, granola, yogurt, or honey

Instructions:

1. In a bowl or jar, combine the chia seeds, milk, sweetener (if using), and vanilla extract. Stir well to combine.
2. Let the mixture sit for a few minutes, then stir again to prevent clumping. Allow it to sit for another 5-10 minutes until it starts to thicken.
3. Once the mixture has thickened, give it a final stir to ensure that the chia seeds are evenly distributed.
4. Cover the bowl or jar and refrigerate the chia pudding for at least 2 hours, or preferably overnight. This allows the chia seeds to absorb the liquid and develop a pudding-like consistency.
5. After chilling, give the chia pudding a stir to loosen it up. If it's too thick, you can add a splash of milk to reach your desired consistency.
6. Divide the chia pudding into serving bowls or jars and add your favorite toppings, such as fresh fruit, nuts, seeds, shredded coconut, granola, yogurt, or honey.
7. Serve the gut-healthy chia pudding immediately and enjoy it as a nutritious breakfast, snack, or dessert!

Feel free to customize this recipe to suit your taste preferences. You can experiment with different types of milk, sweeteners, flavorings, and toppings to create endless variations of gut-healthy chia pudding.

**Gut-Healing Turkey and Rice Congee**

Ingredients:

- 1 cup white rice (jasmine rice or sushi rice works well)
- 8 cups water or low-sodium chicken broth
- 1 pound ground turkey or shredded cooked turkey
- 2 tablespoons ginger, finely minced
- 2 cloves garlic, minced
- 2 tablespoons soy sauce or tamari (use gluten-free if needed)
- 1 tablespoon rice vinegar
- Salt and pepper to taste
- Optional toppings: chopped green onions, cilantro, sliced mushrooms, shredded carrots, bean sprouts, soft-boiled eggs, sesame oil, chili oil

Instructions:

1. Rinse the rice under cold water until the water runs clear. This helps remove excess starch from the rice.
2. In a large pot, bring the water or chicken broth to a boil over medium-high heat. Add the rinsed rice and reduce the heat to low. Let the rice simmer, stirring occasionally, for about 1 hour, or until it reaches a porridge-like consistency. If the congee becomes too thick, you can add more water or broth to thin it out.
3. While the rice is cooking, prepare the turkey. If using ground turkey, cook it in a separate skillet over medium heat until browned and cooked through. If using shredded cooked turkey, simply warm it up in a skillet or microwave.
4. Once the rice has reached the desired consistency, add the cooked turkey to the pot.
5. Stir in the minced ginger, minced garlic, soy sauce or tamari, and rice vinegar. Season with salt and pepper to taste. Let the congee simmer for an additional 10-15 minutes to allow the flavors to meld.
6. Taste the congee and adjust the seasoning if needed. Add more soy sauce, rice vinegar, salt, or pepper according to your taste preferences.
7. Serve the gut-healing turkey and rice congee hot, garnished with your choice of toppings such as chopped green onions, cilantro, sliced mushrooms, shredded carrots, bean sprouts, soft-boiled eggs, sesame oil, or chili oil.

8. Enjoy this comforting and nourishing dish as a light meal or soothing remedy for an upset stomach!

Feel free to customize this recipe by adding other gut-friendly ingredients such as diced vegetables or herbs. Congee is versatile and can be adapted to suit your taste preferences and dietary needs.

**Gut-Friendly Zucchini Noodles with Pesto**

Ingredients:

For the zucchini noodles:

- 4 medium zucchini
- Salt

For the pesto:

- 2 cups fresh basil leaves, packed
- 1/3 cup raw walnuts or pine nuts
- 2 cloves garlic
- 1/4 cup grated Parmesan cheese (optional, omit if dairy-free)
- 1/4 cup extra virgin olive oil
- 1 tablespoon fresh lemon juice
- Salt and pepper to taste

Optional toppings:

- Cherry tomatoes, halved
- Toasted pine nuts or walnuts
- Grated Parmesan cheese (optional)
- Fresh basil leaves, torn

Instructions:

1. Prepare the zucchini noodles:

- Trim the ends of the zucchini and use a spiralizer to create noodles. Alternatively, you can use a julienne peeler or a mandoline slicer with a julienne attachment.

- Place the zucchini noodles in a colander and sprinkle them with salt. Let them sit for about 10-15 minutes to release excess moisture. This step helps prevent the noodles from becoming too watery when cooked.

2. Make the pesto:

- In a food processor, combine the fresh basil leaves, walnuts or pine nuts, garlic, and grated Parmesan cheese (if using). Pulse until the ingredients are finely chopped.
- With the food processor running, slowly drizzle in the extra virgin olive oil and lemon juice until the pesto reaches a smooth and creamy consistency.
- Season the pesto with salt and pepper to taste. Adjust the seasoning as needed.

3. Cook the zucchini noodles:

- After the zucchini noodles have released excess moisture, gently squeeze them to remove any remaining water.
- Heat a large skillet over medium heat. Add a small amount of olive oil or cooking spray to the skillet.
- Add the zucchini noodles to the skillet and sauté them for 2-3 minutes, or until they are just tender but still slightly crisp. Be careful not to overcook them, as they can become mushy.
- Remove the skillet from the heat and add the pesto sauce to the zucchini noodles. Toss until the noodles are evenly coated with the pesto.

4. Serve:

- Divide the zucchini noodles with pesto among serving plates.
- Garnish with cherry tomatoes, toasted pine nuts or walnuts, grated Parmesan cheese (if using), and fresh basil leaves.
- Serve immediately and enjoy your gut-friendly zucchini noodles with pesto!

This dish is light, flavorful, and packed with nutrients, making it a perfect option for anyone looking to support their gut health while enjoying a satisfying meal.

**Fermented Pickles**

Ingredients:

- 4-6 pickling cucumbers (Kirby or Persian cucumbers work well)
- 2-3 cloves garlic, peeled and smashed
- 1-2 tablespoons pickling spices (optional)
- 2 tablespoons pickling salt or sea salt (avoid iodized salt)
- Filtered water
- Fresh dill (optional)
- Grape leaves or oak leaves (optional, for added crispness)

Equipment:

- Quart-sized mason jar or fermentation crock
- Small weight (such as a clean rock or fermentation weight)
- Clean cloth or paper towel
- Rubber band or string

Instructions:

1. Wash the cucumbers thoroughly and trim off any stem ends. You can leave them whole or slice them into spears or rounds, depending on your preference.
2. In the bottom of a clean quart-sized mason jar or fermentation crock, place the smashed garlic cloves, pickling spices (if using), and fresh dill (if using).
3. Pack the cucumbers tightly into the jar or crock, leaving about an inch of space at the top.
4. Dissolve the pickling salt or sea salt in filtered water to create a brine. The ratio is typically 1 tablespoon of salt per quart of water. Pour the brine over the cucumbers, ensuring they are completely submerged. If needed, use a small weight to keep the cucumbers submerged under the brine.
5. If desired, add a grape leaf or oak leaf to the top of the cucumbers. These leaves contain tannins, which can help keep the pickles crisp during fermentation.
6. Cover the jar or crock with a clean cloth or paper towel and secure it with a rubber band or string. This allows airflow while keeping out dust and insects.
7. Place the jar or crock in a cool, dark place to ferment. The ideal temperature for fermentation is between 60-75°F (15-24°C). Fermentation time can vary

depending on temperature and desired level of sourness, but typically takes 1-2 weeks.
8. Check the pickles daily to ensure they remain submerged under the brine. If any scum or mold forms on the surface, simply skim it off with a clean spoon.
9. Taste the pickles after a few days of fermentation. Once they reach your desired level of sourness, transfer the jar to the refrigerator to slow down the fermentation process. The pickles will continue to develop flavor over time.
10. Enjoy your homemade fermented pickles as a tasty snack, sandwich topping, or accompaniment to your favorite dishes!

Experiment with different spices and flavorings to customize your pickles to your taste preferences. Fermented pickles can be stored in the refrigerator for several months, where they will continue to develop flavor.

**Gut-Healing Coconut Curry**

Ingredients:

- 1 tablespoon coconut oil or olive oil
- 1 onion, chopped
- 2 cloves garlic, minced
- 1 tablespoon fresh ginger, grated
- 2 tablespoons curry powder
- 1 teaspoon ground turmeric
- 1 can (14 oz) coconut milk
- 2 cups low-sodium vegetable broth or bone broth
- 2 cups chopped vegetables of your choice (e.g., bell peppers, carrots, broccoli, zucchini)
- 1 cup cooked chickpeas or lentils (optional, for added protein)
- Salt and pepper to taste
- Fresh cilantro, chopped, for garnish
- Cooked rice or quinoa, for serving

Instructions:

1. In a large skillet or pot, heat the coconut oil over medium heat. Add the chopped onion and cook until softened, about 5 minutes.
2. Add the minced garlic and grated ginger to the skillet, and cook for another minute until fragrant.
3. Stir in the curry powder and ground turmeric, and cook for another minute to toast the spices.
4. Pour in the coconut milk and vegetable broth, stirring to combine. Bring the mixture to a simmer.
5. Add the chopped vegetables to the skillet, along with the cooked chickpeas or lentils if using. Stir well to coat the vegetables in the curry sauce.
6. Cover the skillet and let the curry simmer for about 15-20 minutes, or until the vegetables are tender.
7. Taste the curry and season with salt and pepper to taste.
8. Serve the gut-healing coconut curry hot, garnished with fresh chopped cilantro, and accompanied by cooked rice or quinoa.

This gut-healing coconut curry is rich in flavor and nutrients, making it a satisfying and nourishing meal. Feel free to customize the recipe by using your favorite vegetables and adjusting the spice level to suit your taste preferences. Enjoy!

**Gut-Friendly Banana Smoothie Bowl**

Ingredients:

For the smoothie base:

- 2 ripe bananas, peeled and frozen
- 1/2 cup plain Greek yogurt or dairy-free yogurt
- 1/4 cup almond milk or any other milk of your choice
- 1 tablespoon almond butter or peanut butter (optional)
- 1 tablespoon ground flaxseed or chia seeds (optional)

For toppings:

- Sliced bananas
- Fresh berries (such as strawberries, blueberries, or raspberries)
- Granola or toasted oats
- Nuts and seeds (such as almonds, walnuts, pumpkin seeds, or sunflower seeds)
- Shredded coconut
- Honey or maple syrup (optional, for drizzling)

Instructions:

1. In a blender, combine the frozen bananas, Greek yogurt, almond milk, almond butter or peanut butter (if using), and ground flaxseed or chia seeds (if using). Blend until smooth and creamy, adding more almond milk if needed to reach your desired consistency.
2. Pour the smoothie base into a bowl.
3. Arrange your desired toppings on top of the smoothie base. You can be as creative as you like with the toppings, adding a variety of textures and flavors.
4. Drizzle honey or maple syrup on top if desired, for a touch of sweetness.
5. Serve the gut-friendly banana smoothie bowl immediately and enjoy it with a spoon!

This smoothie bowl is not only delicious but also provides a good balance of carbohydrates, protein, healthy fats, and fiber to support gut health. Feel free to customize the recipe with your favorite fruits, nuts, seeds, and other toppings. It's a great way to start your day or enjoy as a refreshing snack!

**Kimchi Pancakes**

Ingredients:

- 1 cup all-purpose flour
- 1 cup kimchi, chopped
- 1/4 cup kimchi juice (liquid from the kimchi jar)
- 2 green onions, thinly sliced
- 1 tablespoon soy sauce
- 1 teaspoon sesame oil
- 1/2 cup water
- 2 tablespoons vegetable oil, for frying

Dipping sauce:

- 2 tablespoons soy sauce
- 1 tablespoon rice vinegar
- 1 teaspoon sesame oil
- 1 teaspoon sesame seeds
- 1 green onion, thinly sliced

Instructions:

1. In a large mixing bowl, combine the flour, chopped kimchi, sliced green onions, soy sauce, sesame oil, and kimchi juice.
2. Gradually add the water while stirring until a thick batter forms. You may not need to use all of the water, depending on the consistency of the batter.
3. Heat a non-stick skillet or frying pan over medium heat and add a tablespoon of vegetable oil.
4. Once the oil is hot, pour a ladleful of the pancake batter into the skillet and spread it out into a thin, even layer.
5. Cook the pancake for 2-3 minutes on each side, or until golden brown and crispy. Use a spatula to flip the pancake carefully.
6. Repeat the process with the remaining batter, adding more oil to the skillet as needed.

7. While the pancakes are cooking, prepare the dipping sauce by combining the soy sauce, rice vinegar, sesame oil, sesame seeds, and sliced green onion in a small bowl.
8. Once all the pancakes are cooked, serve them hot with the dipping sauce on the side.
9. Enjoy your delicious kimchi pancakes as a snack or appetizer!

These kimchi pancakes are crispy on the outside, soft on the inside, and packed with the umami flavor of kimchi. They make a fantastic savory treat that's perfect for any occasion.

**Gut-Healthy Quinoa Salad**

Ingredients:

- 1 cup quinoa, rinsed
- 2 cups water or low-sodium vegetable broth
- 1 can (15 oz) chickpeas, drained and rinsed
- 1 cup cherry tomatoes, halved
- 1 cucumber, diced
- 1 bell pepper, diced (red, yellow, or orange)
- 1/4 cup red onion, finely chopped
- 1/4 cup fresh parsley, chopped
- 1/4 cup fresh cilantro, chopped
- 1/4 cup extra virgin olive oil
- 2 tablespoons apple cider vinegar or lemon juice
- 1 teaspoon Dijon mustard
- 1 clove garlic, minced
- Salt and pepper to taste
- Optional add-ins: diced avocado, chopped spinach, shredded carrots, toasted nuts or seeds, crumbled feta cheese

Instructions:

1. In a medium saucepan, combine the quinoa and water or vegetable broth. Bring to a boil over high heat.
2. Reduce the heat to low, cover, and simmer for 15-20 minutes, or until the quinoa is tender and the liquid is absorbed. Remove from heat and let it cool to room temperature.
3. In a large mixing bowl, combine the cooked quinoa, chickpeas, cherry tomatoes, cucumber, bell pepper, red onion, parsley, and cilantro.
4. In a small bowl, whisk together the extra virgin olive oil, apple cider vinegar or lemon juice, Dijon mustard, minced garlic, salt, and pepper to make the dressing.
5. Pour the dressing over the quinoa salad and toss until everything is evenly coated.
6. Taste and adjust the seasoning if needed. You can add more salt, pepper, or vinegar to suit your taste preferences.
7. If desired, add any optional add-ins such as diced avocado, chopped spinach, shredded carrots, toasted nuts or seeds, or crumbled feta cheese.

8. Serve the gut-healthy quinoa salad immediately at room temperature, or chill it in the refrigerator for at least 30 minutes to allow the flavors to meld before serving.

This quinoa salad is rich in fiber, protein, and healthy fats, making it a satisfying and nutritious meal or side dish. Enjoy!

**Gut-Healing Chicken and Rice Soup**

Ingredients:

- 1 tablespoon olive oil or coconut oil
- 1 onion, diced
- 2 carrots, diced
- 2 celery stalks, diced
- 2 cloves garlic, minced
- 6 cups low-sodium chicken broth or bone broth
- 2 cups cooked shredded chicken (rotisserie chicken works well)
- 1 cup cooked white rice or brown rice
- 1 teaspoon dried thyme
- 1 teaspoon dried rosemary
- Salt and pepper to taste
- Fresh parsley, chopped, for garnish (optional)

Instructions:

1. In a large pot or Dutch oven, heat the olive oil over medium heat. Add the diced onion, carrots, and celery, and cook until softened, about 5-7 minutes.
2. Add the minced garlic to the pot and cook for another minute until fragrant.
3. Pour in the chicken broth or bone broth, and bring the soup to a simmer.
4. Add the shredded chicken, cooked rice, dried thyme, and dried rosemary to the pot. Stir well to combine.
5. Season the soup with salt and pepper to taste. Be mindful of the salt content in your broth, as some varieties can be quite salty.
6. Let the soup simmer for 15-20 minutes to allow the flavors to meld together.
7. Taste the soup and adjust the seasoning if needed. Add more salt, pepper, or herbs to suit your taste preferences.
8. Ladle the gut-healing chicken and rice soup into bowls, and garnish with chopped fresh parsley if desired.
9. Serve the soup hot and enjoy its nourishing and comforting goodness!

This chicken and rice soup is gentle on the digestive system while still providing plenty of nutrients and flavor. It's perfect for anyone looking to support their gut health or enjoy a comforting meal. Feel free to customize the recipe by adding other gut-friendly ingredients like ginger or leafy greens.

**Gut-Friendly Sourdough Pancakes**

Ingredients:

- 1 cup sourdough starter (fed and active)
- 1 cup all-purpose flour or whole wheat flour
- 1 tablespoon maple syrup or honey (optional)
- 1/2 teaspoon baking soda
- 1/4 teaspoon salt
- 1 large egg
- 1 tablespoon melted butter or coconut oil
- Additional butter or oil for cooking
- Optional toppings: fresh fruit, yogurt, nuts, seeds, maple syrup

Instructions:

1. In a large mixing bowl, combine the sourdough starter, flour, and maple syrup or honey (if using). Stir until well combined. The batter will be thick.
2. Cover the bowl with a clean kitchen towel or plastic wrap and let it sit at room temperature overnight or for at least 8 hours. This allows the sourdough starter to ferment the batter, which helps improve its digestibility and flavor.
3. After the fermentation period, the batter will be bubbly and slightly puffy. Preheat a non-stick skillet or griddle over medium heat.
4. In a small bowl, whisk together the baking soda and salt. Sprinkle this mixture over the fermented batter and gently fold it in until well incorporated.
5. In a separate bowl, beat the egg and melted butter or coconut oil together. Add this mixture to the batter and stir until everything is evenly combined.
6. Grease the preheated skillet or griddle with butter or oil. Pour about 1/4 cup of batter onto the skillet for each pancake, spreading it slightly with the back of a spoon to form a round shape.
7. Cook the pancakes for 2-3 minutes, or until bubbles form on the surface and the edges look set. Flip the pancakes and cook for another 1-2 minutes, or until golden brown and cooked through.
8. Transfer the cooked pancakes to a plate and keep them warm while you cook the remaining batter.
9. Serve the gut-friendly sourdough pancakes hot, topped with your favorite toppings such as fresh fruit, yogurt, nuts, seeds, or maple syrup.

These sourdough pancakes are not only delicious but also potentially easier to digest and more gut-friendly due to the fermentation process. Enjoy them as a nutritious breakfast or brunch option!

**Fermented Beet Kvass**

Ingredients:

- 2-3 medium-sized beets, peeled and chopped into small pieces
- 4 cups filtered water (non-chlorinated)
- 1-2 tablespoons sea salt or kosher salt (non-iodized)
- Optional flavorings: ginger slices, garlic cloves, peppercorns, herbs (such as dill or cilantro)

Equipment:

- 1-quart glass jar with a lid
- Clean cloth or paper towel
- Rubber band or string

Instructions:

1. Wash and peel the beets, then chop them into small cubes or slices.
2. Place the chopped beets in the glass jar, filling it about halfway.
3. Dissolve the sea salt or kosher salt in the filtered water to create a brine. Use 1-2 tablespoons of salt per quart of water, depending on your taste preferences for saltiness.
4. Pour the brine over the beets in the jar, making sure they are completely submerged. Leave about an inch of space at the top of the jar.
5. If using any optional flavorings, add them to the jar with the beets and brine.
6. Cover the jar with a clean cloth or paper towel and secure it with a rubber band or string. This allows air to flow while keeping out dust and insects.
7. Place the jar in a cool, dark place (such as a pantry or cupboard) and let it ferment for 3-7 days, depending on the temperature and desired level of fermentation. Warmer temperatures will result in faster fermentation.
8. Check the kvass daily to monitor the fermentation process. You should start to see bubbles forming, indicating that fermentation is taking place.
9. Taste the kvass after a few days to see if it has reached your desired level of fermentation. It should have a tangy, slightly sour flavor. If it's not tangy enough, you can let it ferment for a few more days.

10. Once the kvass has fermented to your liking, strain out the beets and transfer the liquid to a clean glass bottle or jar with a lid.
11. Store the fermented beet kvass in the refrigerator to slow down the fermentation process and chill it before serving.
12. Serve the fermented beet kvass cold as a refreshing and probiotic-rich beverage. Enjoy it on its own or mixed with a splash of sparkling water for a fizzy twist.

Fermented beet kvass can be enjoyed as a tangy and refreshing drink, and it may provide potential health benefits due to its probiotic content.

**Gut-Healing Sweet Potato and Lentil Curry**

Ingredients:

- 1 tablespoon coconut oil or olive oil
- 1 onion, finely chopped
- 2 cloves garlic, minced
- 1 tablespoon fresh ginger, grated
- 2 medium sweet potatoes, peeled and diced
- 1 cup dried red lentils, rinsed
- 1 can (14 oz) coconut milk
- 2 cups vegetable broth or water
- 1 tablespoon curry powder
- 1 teaspoon ground turmeric
- 1 teaspoon ground cumin
- 1/2 teaspoon ground coriander
- 1/4 teaspoon cayenne pepper (optional, adjust to taste)
- Salt and pepper to taste
- Fresh cilantro, chopped, for garnish (optional)
- Cooked rice or quinoa, for serving

Instructions:

1. In a large pot or Dutch oven, heat the coconut oil over medium heat. Add the chopped onion and cook until softened, about 5 minutes.
2. Add the minced garlic and grated ginger to the pot, and cook for another minute until fragrant.
3. Stir in the diced sweet potatoes and rinsed red lentils.
4. Pour in the coconut milk and vegetable broth or water, stirring to combine.
5. Add the curry powder, ground turmeric, ground cumin, ground coriander, and cayenne pepper (if using) to the pot. Stir well to distribute the spices evenly.
6. Season the curry with salt and pepper to taste.
7. Bring the curry to a simmer, then reduce the heat to low and cover the pot. Let the curry cook for 20-25 minutes, or until the sweet potatoes and lentils are tender, stirring occasionally.
8. Taste the curry and adjust the seasoning if needed. Add more salt, pepper, or spices according to your taste preferences.

9. Serve the gut-healing sweet potato and lentil curry hot, garnished with fresh chopped cilantro if desired.
10. Enjoy the curry with cooked rice or quinoa for a complete and satisfying meal.

This gut-healing sweet potato and lentil curry is rich in fiber, protein, and anti-inflammatory spices, making it a comforting and nourishing dish for supporting digestive health. Feel free to customize the recipe by adding other gut-friendly ingredients like leafy greens or diced vegetables.

**Gut-Friendly Overnight Chia Seed Pudding**

Ingredients:

- 1/4 cup chia seeds
- 1 cup unsweetened almond milk, coconut milk, or any other milk of your choice
- 1-2 tablespoons maple syrup, honey, or other sweetener of your choice (optional)
- 1/2 teaspoon vanilla extract
- Optional toppings: fresh fruit (e.g., berries, banana slices), nuts, seeds, shredded coconut, granola, yogurt, or honey

Instructions:

1. In a bowl or jar, combine the chia seeds, milk, sweetener (if using), and vanilla extract. Stir well to combine.
2. Let the mixture sit for a few minutes, then stir again to prevent clumping. Allow it to sit for another 5-10 minutes until it starts to thicken.
3. Once the mixture has thickened, give it a final stir to ensure that the chia seeds are evenly distributed.
4. Cover the bowl or jar and refrigerate the chia pudding for at least 2 hours, or preferably overnight. This allows the chia seeds to absorb the liquid and develop a pudding-like consistency.
5. After chilling, give the chia pudding a stir to loosen it up. If it's too thick, you can add a splash of milk to reach your desired consistency.
6. Divide the chia pudding into serving bowls or jars and add your favorite toppings, such as fresh fruit, nuts, seeds, shredded coconut, granola, yogurt, or honey.
7. Serve the gut-friendly overnight chia seed pudding immediately and enjoy it as a nutritious breakfast, snack, or dessert!

Feel free to customize this recipe to suit your taste preferences. You can experiment with different types of milk, sweeteners, flavorings, and toppings to create endless variations of gut-friendly chia seed pudding.

**Gut-Healthy Roasted Brussels Sprouts**

Ingredients:

- 1 pound Brussels sprouts
- 2 tablespoons olive oil or avocado oil
- Salt and pepper to taste

Optional seasoning:

- Garlic powder
- Onion powder
- Paprika
- Lemon zest
- Balsamic vinegar

Instructions:

1. Preheat your oven to 400°F (200°C) and line a baking sheet with parchment paper or aluminum foil for easy cleanup
2. Rinse the Brussels sprouts under cold water and pat them dry with a kitchen towel. Trim off the ends and remove any discolored outer leaves.
3. Cut the Brussels sprouts in half lengthwise and place them in a large mixing bowl.
4. Drizzle the olive oil or avocado oil over the Brussels sprouts and toss to coat them evenly. Season with salt and pepper to taste, along with any optional seasoning of your choice.
5. Arrange the Brussels sprouts in a single layer on the prepared baking sheet, cut side down.
6. Roast the Brussels sprouts in the preheated oven for 20-25 minutes, or until they are tender and caramelized, stirring halfway through the cooking time for even browning.
7. Once the Brussels sprouts are done roasting, remove them from the oven and transfer them to a serving dish.
8. Serve the gut-healthy roasted Brussels sprouts hot as a delicious side dish or snack.

Roasting Brussels sprouts brings out their natural sweetness and enhances their flavor, making them a tasty and nutritious addition to any meal. Enjoy these gut-healthy roasted Brussels sprouts on their own or paired with your favorite protein and grains for a complete and satisfying dish!

**Gut-Healing Turmeric Golden Milk**

Ingredients:

- 1 cup unsweetened almond milk, coconut milk, or any other milk of your choice
- 1 teaspoon ground turmeric
- 1/2 teaspoon ground cinnamon
- 1/4 teaspoon ground ginger
- 1/8 teaspoon ground black pepper
- 1 teaspoon coconut oil or ghee (optional, for added creaminess)
- 1 teaspoon honey, maple syrup, or other sweetener of your choice (optional, adjust to taste)
- Pinch of ground nutmeg (optional, for garnish)
- Pinch of ground cardamom (optional, for garnish)

Instructions:

1. In a small saucepan, heat the milk over medium heat until it starts to steam but is not boiling.
2. Whisk in the ground turmeric, ground cinnamon, ground ginger, ground black pepper, and coconut oil or ghee (if using).
3. Continue to heat the mixture for another 2-3 minutes, stirring occasionally, until it is warmed through and fragrant.
4. Remove the saucepan from the heat and sweeten the golden milk with honey, maple syrup, or another sweetener of your choice, adjusting to taste.
5. Pour the turmeric golden milk into a mug and sprinkle with a pinch of ground nutmeg and ground cardamom for garnish, if desired.
6. Stir the golden milk well before serving to ensure that the spices are evenly distributed.
7. Enjoy your gut-healing turmeric golden milk warm and sip it slowly to experience its soothing and comforting effects.

Turmeric golden milk is a delicious and nourishing beverage that can be enjoyed any time of day, but is especially comforting as a nighttime drink before bed. The combination of turmeric and spices provides potential health benefits, while the warmth of the milk makes it a cozy treat for the digestive system. Adjust the sweetness and spice levels to suit your taste preferences, and feel free to customize the recipe with other gut-friendly ingredients like ginger or cinnamon.

**Fermented Carrots**

Ingredients:

- 1 pound carrots, peeled and cut into sticks or rounds
- 2-3 cloves garlic, peeled and smashed (optional)
- 1 tablespoon sea salt or kosher salt (non-iodized)
- Filtered water

Optional seasonings:

- Fresh dill
- Whole black peppercorns
- Mustard seeds
- Red pepper flakes
- Ginger slices

Equipment:

- Clean quart-sized glass jar with a lid
- Small weight (such as a clean rock or fermentation weight)
- Clean cloth or paper towel
- Rubber band or string

Instructions:

1. Wash and peel the carrots, then cut them into sticks or rounds. Pack the carrots tightly into the glass jar, leaving about an inch of space at the top.
2. If using, add the smashed garlic cloves and any other optional seasonings to the jar with the carrots.
3. In a separate bowl, dissolve the sea salt or kosher salt in filtered water to create a brine. The ratio is typically 1 tablespoon of salt per quart of water.
4. Pour the brine over the carrots in the jar, making sure they are completely submerged. Leave about an inch of space between the brine and the top of the jar.

5. Place a small weight on top of the carrots to keep them submerged under the brine. This helps prevent mold growth.
6. Cover the jar with a clean cloth or paper towel and secure it with a rubber band or string. This allows air to flow while keeping out dust and insects.
7. Place the jar in a cool, dark place (such as a pantry or cupboard) and let it ferment for 3-7 days, depending on the temperature and desired level of fermentation. Warmer temperatures will result in faster fermentation.
8. Check the carrots daily to monitor the fermentation process. You should start to see bubbles forming, indicating that fermentation is taking place.
9. Taste the fermented carrots after a few days to see if they have reached your desired level of tanginess. Once they have fermented to your liking, transfer the jar to the refrigerator to slow down the fermentation process.
10. Enjoy the fermented carrots as a crunchy and tangy snack, or use them as a flavorful addition to salads, sandwiches, or Buddha bowls.

Fermented carrots can be stored in the refrigerator for several weeks, where they will continue to develop flavor. Enjoy their probiotic-rich goodness as part of your daily diet to support gut health!

**Gut-Friendly Coconut Kefir**

Ingredients:

- 1 can (14 oz) full-fat coconut milk (unsweetened)
- 1-2 tablespoons milk kefir grains or a kefir starter culture

Instructions:

1. Sterilize a glass jar and utensils by washing them with hot, soapy water and rinsing them thoroughly.
2. Pour the coconut milk into the glass jar.
3. Add the milk kefir grains or kefir starter culture to the coconut milk and stir gently to combine.
4. Cover the jar loosely with a clean cloth or paper towel and secure it with a rubber band or string. This allows air to flow while keeping out dust and insects.
5. Place the jar in a warm spot, away from direct sunlight. The ideal temperature for fermenting coconut kefir is between 70-75°F (21-24°C).
6. Let the coconut kefir ferment for 12-48 hours, depending on the desired level of tartness. The longer you ferment it, the tangier it will become. Stir the mixture occasionally during the fermentation process.
7. After the fermentation period, the coconut kefir should have a slightly tangy flavor and a thicker consistency.
8. Strain out the milk kefir grains, if using, using a non-metal strainer. You can reuse the grains to make another batch of coconut kefir.
9. Transfer the strained coconut kefir to a clean glass jar or bottle with a tight-fitting lid.
10. Store the coconut kefir in the refrigerator to slow down the fermentation process and chill it before serving.
11. Enjoy your gut-friendly coconut kefir cold as a refreshing beverage or use it in smoothies, salad dressings, or other recipes.

Coconut kefir is a delicious and nutritious probiotic-rich drink that can help support gut health. It's a great dairy-free alternative to traditional milk kefir and can be enjoyed by those with lactose intolerance or dairy sensitivities. Experiment with different flavors and variations by adding fruit, herbs, or spices to customize your coconut kefir to your taste preferences.

**Gut-Healing Vegetable Broth**

Ingredients:

- 2 large carrots, chopped
- 2 celery stalks, chopped
- 1 onion, chopped
- 1 leek, chopped (optional)
- 4 cloves garlic, smashed
- 1-inch piece of ginger, sliced
- 1 bunch parsley
- 1 handful spinach or kale leaves
- 1 tablespoon whole peppercorns
- 2 bay leaves
- 8-10 cups water

Optional add-ins for extra gut health benefits:

- 1 tablespoon apple cider vinegar (helps extract minerals from vegetables)
- 1 tablespoon turmeric powder (anti-inflammatory)
- 1 tablespoon dried seaweed (for added minerals)
- 1 tablespoon miso paste (probiotic-rich)

Instructions:

1. In a large pot, combine all the chopped vegetables, herbs, and spices.
2. Add water to cover the vegetables by about an inch.
3. Optional: Add apple cider vinegar to help extract minerals from the vegetables.
4. Bring the pot to a boil over high heat, then reduce the heat to low and let the broth simmer uncovered for 1-2 hours.
5. As the broth simmers, skim off any foam that rises to the surface with a spoon.
6. After simmering, remove the pot from the heat and let the broth cool slightly.
7. Strain the broth through a fine-mesh sieve or cheesecloth into a large bowl or container, discarding the solids.
8. Optional: Stir in turmeric powder, dried seaweed, or miso paste for added gut health benefits and flavor.

9. Let the broth cool completely before storing it in the refrigerator or freezer.
10. Use the gut-healing vegetable broth as a base for soups, stews, sauces, or to sip on its own as a nourishing beverage.

This gut-healing vegetable broth is rich in vitamins, minerals, and antioxidants, making it a soothing and nourishing addition to your diet. Feel free to customize the recipe by adding your favorite vegetables and herbs, or adjust the seasoning to suit your taste preferences.

**Gut-Friendly Chickpea Salad**

Ingredients:

- 2 cans (15 oz each) chickpeas, drained and rinsed
- 1 cucumber, diced
- 1 bell pepper (any color), diced
- 1/4 red onion, finely chopped
- 1/4 cup fresh parsley, chopped
- 1/4 cup fresh cilantro, chopped
- Juice of 1 lemon
- 2 tablespoons extra virgin olive oil
- 1 teaspoon ground cumin
- 1/2 teaspoon paprika
- Salt and pepper to taste
- Optional add-ins: cherry tomatoes, olives, avocado, feta cheese, diced jalapeño

Instructions:

1. In a large mixing bowl, combine the drained and rinsed chickpeas, diced cucumber, diced bell pepper, finely chopped red onion, chopped parsley, and chopped cilantro.
2. In a small bowl, whisk together the lemon juice, extra virgin olive oil, ground cumin, paprika, salt, and pepper to make the dressing.
3. Pour the dressing over the chickpea salad and toss until everything is evenly coated.
4. Taste the salad and adjust the seasoning if needed. Add more salt, pepper, or lemon juice to suit your taste preferences.
5. If desired, add any optional add-ins such as halved cherry tomatoes, sliced olives, diced avocado, crumbled feta cheese, or diced jalapeño for extra flavor and texture.
6. Let the chickpea salad sit at room temperature for about 15-30 minutes to allow the flavors to meld together.
7. Serve the gut-friendly chickpea salad chilled or at room temperature as a nutritious side dish or light meal.

This chickpea salad is not only gut-friendly but also versatile and easy to customize with your favorite ingredients. Enjoy it as a healthy lunch option, pack it for picnics or potlucks, or serve it alongside grilled meats or fish for a complete and satisfying meal.

**Gut-Healthy Roasted Cauliflower**

Ingredients:

- 1 large head of cauliflower, cut into florets
- 2-3 tablespoons olive oil or avocado oil
- 2 cloves garlic, minced
- 1 teaspoon ground cumin
- 1/2 teaspoon smoked paprika
- Salt and pepper to taste
- Fresh parsley or cilantro, chopped (optional, for garnish)

Instructions:

1. Preheat your oven to 425°F (220°C) and line a baking sheet with parchment paper or aluminum foil for easy cleanup.
2. In a large mixing bowl, combine the cauliflower florets with olive oil, minced garlic, ground cumin, smoked paprika, salt, and pepper. Toss until the cauliflower is evenly coated with the seasonings.
3. Spread the seasoned cauliflower florets out in a single layer on the prepared baking sheet, making sure they are not overcrowded. This allows them to roast evenly and become crispy.
4. Roast the cauliflower in the preheated oven for 25-30 minutes, or until golden brown and tender, stirring halfway through the cooking time for even browning.
5. Once the cauliflower is roasted to your desired level of crispiness, remove it from the oven and transfer it to a serving dish.
6. Garnish the roasted cauliflower with chopped fresh parsley or cilantro, if desired, for a pop of color and freshness.
7. Serve the gut-healthy roasted cauliflower hot as a delicious side dish or appetizer.

Roasted cauliflower is a versatile dish that pairs well with a variety of main courses and can be enjoyed on its own as a tasty snack. It's naturally low in calories and carbohydrates, making it suitable for many dietary preferences. Plus, cauliflower is rich in fiber and antioxidants, which can support gut health and overall well-being. Enjoy this flavorful and nutritious dish as part of your regular meal rotation!

**Fermented Cabbage Kimchi**

Ingredients:

- 1 medium head Napa cabbage (about 2 pounds)
- 1/4 cup sea salt or kosher salt
- Water (for soaking cabbage)
- 1 tablespoon grated ginger
- 3 cloves garlic, minced
- 2 tablespoons fish sauce or soy sauce (for vegan version)
- 2 tablespoons Korean red pepper flakes (gochugaru)
- 2 teaspoons granulated sugar or honey
- 4 green onions, chopped
- 1 medium carrot, julienned (optional)
- 1 daikon radish, julienned (optional)

Instructions:

1. Rinse the Napa cabbage under cold water and remove any damaged outer leaves. Cut the cabbage lengthwise into quarters, then chop it into bite-sized pieces.
2. In a large mixing bowl, dissolve the sea salt or kosher salt in water to create a brine. Submerge the chopped cabbage in the brine, making sure it's fully covered. Let it soak for 1-2 hours, tossing occasionally.
3. While the cabbage is soaking, prepare the seasoning paste. In a small bowl, combine the grated ginger, minced garlic, fish sauce or soy sauce, Korean red pepper flakes, and granulated sugar or honey. Mix until well combined.
4. Rinse the cabbage under cold water to remove excess salt, then drain it thoroughly and squeeze out any excess moisture.
5. In a large mixing bowl, combine the drained cabbage with the seasoning paste, chopped green onions, and any optional julienned carrots or daikon radish. Toss until the cabbage is evenly coated with the seasoning mixture.
6. Pack the seasoned cabbage tightly into clean glass jars or fermentation crocks, pressing down firmly to remove air pockets.
7. Leave about an inch of space at the top of the jars or crocks to allow for expansion during fermentation.
8. Cover the jars or crocks loosely with lids or clean kitchen towels, securing them with rubber bands or string.

9. Place the jars or crocks in a cool, dark place (such as a pantry or cupboard) and let them ferment at room temperature for 3-5 days, depending on your taste preferences.
10. Check the kimchi daily to monitor the fermentation process. Press down on the cabbage with a clean spoon to submerge it under the brine.
11. Once the kimchi reaches your desired level of fermentation, transfer the jars or crocks to the refrigerator to slow down the fermentation process and chill the kimchi before serving.
12. Enjoy your homemade fermented cabbage kimchi as a flavorful condiment or side dish!

Fermented cabbage kimchi is a versatile and delicious addition to meals, providing probiotics and unique flavors. Adjust the seasoning to suit your taste preferences, and feel free to experiment with different vegetables and spices to create your own variations of this traditional Korean dish.

**Gut-Healing Ginger Tea**

Ingredients:

- 1-inch piece of fresh ginger root, thinly sliced or grated
- 2 cups water
- Juice of half a lemon (optional)
- Honey or maple syrup to taste (optional)

Instructions:

1. Peel the ginger root and thinly slice it or grate it using a fine grater.
2. In a small saucepan, bring the water to a boil over medium-high heat.
3. Add the sliced or grated ginger to the boiling water.
4. Reduce the heat to low and let the ginger simmer in the water for about 10-15 minutes, allowing the flavors to infuse.
5. After simmering, remove the saucepan from the heat and let the ginger tea cool slightly.
6. Optional: Stir in the juice of half a lemon for added flavor and a boost of vitamin C.
7. Sweeten the ginger tea with honey or maple syrup to taste, if desired. Both honey and maple syrup have potential prebiotic properties, which can support gut health.
8. Strain the ginger tea through a fine-mesh sieve or cheesecloth into mugs to remove the ginger pieces.
9. Serve the gut-healing ginger tea hot and enjoy its soothing and comforting effects.

Ginger tea is a warming and comforting beverage that can help alleviate digestive discomfort, such as bloating, gas, and nausea. It's also rich in antioxidants and anti-inflammatory compounds, which can further support gut health and overall well-being. Enjoy a cup of homemade ginger tea whenever you need a calming and digestive-friendly drink!

**Gut-Friendly Spaghetti Squash with Marinara Sauce**

Ingredients:

- 1 medium spaghetti squash
- 2 cups marinara sauce (homemade or store-bought)
- 2 tablespoons olive oil
- 2 cloves garlic, minced
- Salt and pepper to taste
- Fresh basil leaves, chopped, for garnish (optional)
- Grated Parmesan cheese or nutritional yeast (for vegan option), for serving (optional)

Instructions:

1. Preheat your oven to 400°F (200°C). Line a baking sheet with parchment paper for easy cleanup.
2. Using a sharp knife, carefully cut the spaghetti squash in half lengthwise. Scoop out the seeds and stringy pulp from the center using a spoon.
3. Drizzle the cut sides of the spaghetti squash halves with olive oil and season with salt and pepper to taste.
4. Place the spaghetti squash halves cut side down on the prepared baking sheet.
5. Roast the spaghetti squash in the preheated oven for 35-45 minutes, or until the flesh is tender and easily pierced with a fork.
6. While the spaghetti squash is roasting, prepare the marinara sauce. In a saucepan, heat the olive oil over medium heat. Add the minced garlic and cook for 1-2 minutes, or until fragrant.
7. Pour the marinara sauce into the saucepan with the garlic and stir to combine. Reduce the heat to low and let the sauce simmer gently while the spaghetti squash finishes roasting.
8. Once the spaghetti squash is done roasting, remove it from the oven and let it cool slightly.
9. Use a fork to scrape the flesh of the spaghetti squash into spaghetti-like strands. Transfer the spaghetti squash strands to a serving dish.
10. Pour the marinara sauce over the spaghetti squash and toss to coat evenly.
11. Garnish the gut-friendly spaghetti squash with chopped fresh basil leaves, if desired.

12. Serve the spaghetti squash with marinara sauce hot, topped with grated Parmesan cheese or nutritional yeast for a cheesy finish, if desired.

This gut-friendly spaghetti squash with marinara sauce is a nutritious and satisfying dish that's perfect for those looking to reduce their carbohydrate intake or incorporate more vegetables into their diet. Enjoy it as a light lunch or dinner option, or serve it as a side dish alongside your favorite protein.

**Gut-Healthy Almond Butter Smoothie**

Ingredients:

- 1 ripe banana, frozen
- 1 tablespoon almond butter
- 1 cup unsweetened almond milk or any milk of your choice
- 1/2 cup plain Greek yogurt or dairy-free yogurt for a vegan option
- 1 tablespoon ground flaxseed or chia seeds
- 1/2 teaspoon ground cinnamon
- Optional sweetener: 1-2 teaspoons honey, maple syrup, or agave syrup (adjust to taste)
- Handful of spinach or kale leaves (optional, for added greens)

Instructions:

1. Add all the ingredients to a blender.
2. Blend on high speed until smooth and creamy, scraping down the sides of the blender as needed to ensure all ingredients are well incorporated.
3. Taste the smoothie and adjust the sweetness if needed by adding more honey, maple syrup, or agave syrup.
4. If you prefer a thinner consistency, you can add more almond milk or water until you reach your desired thickness.
5. Pour the gut-healthy almond butter smoothie into glasses and serve immediately.
6. Optionally, you can garnish the smoothie with a sprinkle of ground cinnamon or a few almond slices for added texture and flavor.
7. Enjoy your gut-friendly almond butter smoothie as a nutritious breakfast, snack, or post-workout refuel!

This almond butter smoothie is rich in protein, fiber, and healthy fats, making it a satisfying and nourishing option for supporting gut health. Feel free to customize the recipe by adding your favorite fruits, vegetables, or additional protein sources like protein powder or hemp seeds.

**Fermented Garlic Dill Pickles**

Ingredients:

- 1 pound pickling cucumbers (Kirby cucumbers), washed
- 2-3 cloves garlic, peeled and smashed
- 2-3 sprigs fresh dill
- 1 tablespoon whole black peppercorns
- 1 tablespoon whole mustard seeds
- 2 tablespoons sea salt or kosher salt (non-iodized)
- Filtered water

Instructions:

1. Wash the pickling cucumbers thoroughly under cold water and trim off the blossom end of each cucumber. The blossom end contains enzymes that can lead to soft pickles.
2. In a clean quart-sized glass jar, add the smashed garlic cloves, fresh dill sprigs, black peppercorns, and mustard seeds.
3. Pack the pickling cucumbers tightly into the jar, leaving about an inch of space from the top.
4. In a separate bowl, dissolve the sea salt or kosher salt in filtered water to create a brine. The ratio is typically 1 tablespoon of salt per quart of water.
5. Pour the brine over the cucumbers in the jar, making sure they are fully submerged. Leave about an inch of space from the top of the jar to allow for expansion during fermentation.
6. Place a weight on top of the cucumbers to keep them submerged under the brine. This helps prevent mold growth.
7. Cover the jar loosely with a clean cloth or paper towel and secure it with a rubber band or string. This allows air to flow while keeping out dust and insects.
8. Place the jar in a cool, dark place (such as a pantry or cupboard) and let it ferment at room temperature for 3-7 days, depending on your taste preferences and the ambient temperature. Warmer temperatures will result in faster fermentation.
9. Check the pickles daily to monitor the fermentation process. You should start to see bubbles forming, indicating that fermentation is taking place.

10. Taste the pickles after a few days to see if they have reached your desired level of tanginess. Once they have fermented to your liking, transfer the jar to the refrigerator to slow down the fermentation process.
11. Enjoy your homemade fermented garlic dill pickles as a tasty and gut-friendly snack or condiment!

These fermented garlic dill pickles will develop a complex flavor profile as they ferment, and they'll be packed with gut-healthy probiotics. Adjust the seasoning and fermentation time to suit your taste preferences, and feel free to experiment with different herbs and spices to create your own variations.

## Gut-Healing Chicken and Vegetable Stir-Fry

Ingredients:

- 2 boneless, skinless chicken breasts, thinly sliced
- 2 tablespoons olive oil or avocado oil
- 2 cloves garlic, minced
- 1-inch piece of ginger, grated
- 2 cups mixed vegetables (such as bell peppers, broccoli, snap peas, carrots, and mushrooms), thinly sliced or chopped
- 2 tablespoons soy sauce or tamari (for gluten-free option)
- 1 tablespoon honey or maple syrup
- 1 tablespoon rice vinegar
- Salt and pepper to taste
- Cooked rice or quinoa, for serving (optional)
- Sesame seeds and chopped green onions for garnish (optional)

Instructions:

1. Heat one tablespoon of oil in a large skillet or wok over medium-high heat. Add the sliced chicken breasts and cook until browned and cooked through, about 5-7 minutes. Remove the chicken from the skillet and set it aside.
2. In the same skillet, add the remaining tablespoon of oil. Add the minced garlic and grated ginger, and cook for 1-2 minutes until fragrant.
3. Add the mixed vegetables to the skillet and stir-fry for 5-7 minutes, or until they are tender-crisp.
4. In a small bowl, whisk together the soy sauce or tamari, honey or maple syrup, and rice vinegar to make the sauce.
5. Return the cooked chicken to the skillet with the vegetables. Pour the sauce over the chicken and vegetables, and toss everything together until evenly coated. Cook for an additional 2-3 minutes to heat through.
6. Season the stir-fry with salt and pepper to taste.
7. Serve the gut-healing chicken and vegetable stir-fry hot, over cooked rice or quinoa if desired.
8. Garnish with sesame seeds and chopped green onions for extra flavor and texture.

This gut-healing chicken and vegetable stir-fry is packed with protein, fiber, vitamins, and minerals, making it a nutritious and satisfying meal. Feel free to customize the recipe by using your favorite vegetables or adding additional spices and seasonings to suit your taste preferences. Enjoy this flavorful and wholesome dish as part of a balanced diet for optimal gut health!

**Gut-Friendly Buckwheat Pancakes**

Ingredients:

- 1 cup buckwheat flour
- 1 tablespoon ground flaxseed (optional, for extra fiber)
- 1 teaspoon baking powder
- 1/4 teaspoon baking soda
- Pinch of salt
- 1 tablespoon honey or maple syrup
- 1 cup unsweetened almond milk or any milk of your choice
- 1 egg (or flaxseed egg for vegan option)
- 1 tablespoon melted coconut oil or olive oil
- Additional oil or cooking spray for greasing the skillet

Instructions:

1. In a large mixing bowl, whisk together the buckwheat flour, ground flaxseed (if using), baking powder, baking soda, and salt.
2. In a separate bowl, whisk together the honey or maple syrup, almond milk, egg, and melted coconut oil or olive oil.
3. Pour the wet ingredients into the dry ingredients and stir until just combined. Be careful not to overmix; a few lumps in the batter are okay.
4. Let the batter rest for about 5-10 minutes to allow the baking powder to activate and the batter to thicken slightly.
5. Heat a non-stick skillet or griddle over medium heat. Lightly grease the skillet with oil or cooking spray.
6. Pour about 1/4 cup of batter onto the skillet for each pancake, spreading it out slightly with the back of a spoon.
7. Cook the pancakes for 2-3 minutes, or until bubbles form on the surface and the edges begin to look set.
8. Carefully flip the pancakes with a spatula and cook for an additional 1-2 minutes on the other side, or until golden brown and cooked through.
9. Transfer the cooked pancakes to a plate and cover them with a clean kitchen towel to keep them warm while you cook the remaining pancakes.
10. Serve the gut-friendly buckwheat pancakes warm with your favorite toppings, such as fresh fruit, yogurt, nut butter, or pure maple syrup.

These gut-friendly buckwheat pancakes are delicious, nutritious, and easy to make. They're a great option for those with gluten sensitivities or anyone looking to add more whole grains to their diet. Enjoy them for breakfast, brunch, or even as a healthy snack!

**Gut-Healthy Roasted Beet Salad**

Ingredients:

- 3-4 medium beets, washed and trimmed
- 2 tablespoons olive oil
- Salt and pepper to taste
- 4 cups mixed salad greens (such as spinach, arugula, or mixed baby greens)
- 1/4 cup crumbled goat cheese or feta cheese (optional, omit for dairy-free or vegan)
- 1/4 cup chopped walnuts or pecans, toasted
- Balsamic glaze or vinaigrette dressing for drizzling (optional)

Instructions:

1. Preheat your oven to 400°F (200°C). Line a baking sheet with parchment paper or aluminum foil for easy cleanup.
2. Wash the beets thoroughly under cold water and trim off the tops and tails. Pat them dry with a clean kitchen towel.
3. Place the whole beets on the prepared baking sheet and drizzle them with olive oil. Use your hands to rub the oil evenly over the beets. Season with salt and pepper to taste.
4. Roast the beets in the preheated oven for 45-60 minutes, or until they are tender when pierced with a fork. The cooking time will depend on the size of the beets.
5. Once the beets are roasted and tender, remove them from the oven and let them cool slightly.
6. While the beets are cooling, prepare the salad greens by washing and drying them thoroughly. Place them in a large mixing bowl.
7. Once the beets are cool enough to handle, use a paper towel or your fingers to peel off the skins. They should come off easily.
8. Cut the roasted beets into bite-sized pieces and add them to the bowl with the salad greens.
9. If using, sprinkle the crumbled goat cheese or feta cheese and toasted chopped nuts over the salad.
10. Drizzle the salad with balsamic glaze or your favorite vinaigrette dressing, if desired, for extra flavor.
11. Toss the salad gently to combine all the ingredients.

12. Serve the gut-healthy roasted beet salad immediately as a delicious and nutritious side dish or light meal.

This roasted beet salad is flavorful, satisfying, and perfect for any occasion. The combination of roasted beets, mixed greens, cheese, and nuts creates a delightful balance of flavors and textures. Enjoy this gut-friendly salad as a refreshing addition to your meal!

**Fermented Jalapeno Hot Sauce**

Ingredients:

- 1 pound jalapeno peppers, stemmed and halved
- 4 cloves garlic, peeled
- 1 small onion, chopped
- 1 tablespoon sea salt or kosher salt (non-iodized)
- 2 cups filtered water
- Fermentation weight or clean rock
- Clean quart-sized glass jar with a lid
- Blender or food processor

Instructions:

1. Wash the jalapeno peppers thoroughly under cold water and remove the stems. Cut them in half lengthwise and remove the seeds if you prefer a milder hot sauce.
2. In a clean quart-sized glass jar, layer the halved jalapeno peppers, peeled garlic cloves, and chopped onion.
3. In a separate bowl, dissolve the sea salt or kosher salt in filtered water to create a brine. The ratio is typically 1 tablespoon of salt per quart of water.
4. Pour the brine over the ingredients in the jar, making sure they are fully submerged. Leave about an inch of space from the top of the jar to allow for expansion during fermentation.
5. Place a fermentation weight or clean rock on top of the ingredients to keep them submerged under the brine. This helps prevent mold growth.
6. Cover the jar loosely with a clean cloth or paper towel and secure it with a rubber band or string. This allows air to flow while keeping out dust and insects.
7. Place the jar in a cool, dark place (such as a pantry or cupboard) and let it ferment at room temperature for 5-7 days, depending on your taste preferences and the ambient temperature. Warmer temperatures will result in faster fermentation.
8. Check the jalapeno peppers daily to monitor the fermentation process. You should start to see bubbles forming, indicating that fermentation is taking place.
9. After 5-7 days, the jalapeno peppers should be soft and slightly tangy from fermentation.

10. Transfer the fermented jalapeno peppers and brine to a blender or food processor. Blend until smooth and creamy, adding a little filtered water if needed to reach your desired consistency.
11. Pour the blended hot sauce into clean glass bottles or jars with tight-fitting lids.
12. Store the fermented jalapeno hot sauce in the refrigerator, where it will continue to develop flavor over time.
13. Enjoy your homemade fermented jalapeno hot sauce as a flavorful and probiotic-rich condiment for tacos, burritos, eggs, and more!

Feel free to customize the recipe by adding other ingredients like lime juice, cilantro, or spices to create your own unique variation of fermented jalapeno hot sauce. Adjust the fermentation time and amount of salt to suit your taste preferences.

**Gut-Healing Turmeric Chicken Soup**

Ingredients:

- 1 tablespoon olive oil or avocado oil
- 1 onion, chopped
- 3 cloves garlic, minced
- 1-inch piece of ginger, grated
- 2 carrots, sliced
- 2 celery stalks, sliced
- 1 teaspoon ground turmeric
- 1/2 teaspoon ground cumin
- 1/2 teaspoon ground coriander
- 1/4 teaspoon cayenne pepper (optional, for added heat)
- 6 cups chicken or vegetable broth
- 2 cups cooked shredded chicken (rotisserie chicken works well)
- 1 cup spinach or kale leaves, chopped
- Juice of 1 lemon
- Salt and pepper to taste
- Fresh cilantro or parsley, chopped, for garnish (optional)

Instructions:

1. Heat the olive oil in a large pot over medium heat. Add the chopped onion and cook for 3-4 minutes, or until translucent.
2. Add the minced garlic and grated ginger to the pot and cook for an additional 1-2 minutes, or until fragrant.
3. Add the sliced carrots and celery to the pot and cook for 5-7 minutes, or until slightly softened.
4. Stir in the ground turmeric, ground cumin, ground coriander, and cayenne pepper (if using) until the vegetables are evenly coated with the spices.
5. Pour the chicken or vegetable broth into the pot and bring the soup to a simmer.
6. Add the cooked shredded chicken to the pot and simmer for 10-15 minutes to allow the flavors to meld together.
7. Stir in the chopped spinach or kale leaves and cook for an additional 2-3 minutes, or until wilted.

8. Remove the pot from the heat and stir in the lemon juice. Season the soup with salt and pepper to taste.
9. Ladle the gut-healing turmeric chicken soup into bowls and garnish with chopped fresh cilantro or parsley, if desired.
10. Serve the turmeric chicken soup hot as a comforting and nourishing meal.

This gut-healing turmeric chicken soup is rich in flavor and loaded with nutritious ingredients that can help support gut health and overall well-being. Enjoy it as a warming meal on chilly days or whenever you need a nourishing pick-me-up!

**Gut-Friendly Coconut Flour Banana Bread**

Ingredients:

- 4 ripe bananas, mashed
- 4 eggs
- 1/4 cup coconut oil, melted
- 1/4 cup honey or maple syrup
- 1 teaspoon vanilla extract
- 1/2 cup coconut flour
- 1 teaspoon baking powder
- 1/2 teaspoon baking soda
- 1/2 teaspoon ground cinnamon
- Pinch of salt
- Optional add-ins: chopped nuts, chocolate chips, dried fruit

Instructions:

1. Preheat your oven to 350°F (175°C). Grease a 9x5-inch loaf pan or line it with parchment paper for easy removal.
2. In a large mixing bowl, mash the ripe bananas with a fork until smooth.
3. Add the eggs, melted coconut oil, honey or maple syrup, and vanilla extract to the mashed bananas. Whisk together until well combined.
4. In a separate bowl, sift together the coconut flour, baking powder, baking soda, ground cinnamon, and salt.
5. Gradually add the dry ingredients to the wet ingredients, stirring until just combined. Be careful not to overmix; a few lumps in the batter are okay.
6. If using any optional add-ins such as chopped nuts, chocolate chips, or dried fruit, fold them into the batter gently.
7. Pour the batter into the prepared loaf pan and spread it out evenly.
8. Bake the coconut flour banana bread in the preheated oven for 50-60 minutes, or until a toothpick inserted into the center comes out clean and the top is golden brown.
9. Remove the banana bread from the oven and let it cool in the pan for 10-15 minutes before transferring it to a wire rack to cool completely.
10. Once cooled, slice the gut-friendly coconut flour banana bread and serve.

This coconut flour banana bread is moist, flavorful, and perfect for breakfast, snack, or dessert. It's naturally sweetened with ripe bananas and honey or maple syrup, making it a healthier alternative to traditional banana bread recipes. Enjoy it on its own or with a spread of nut butter for extra protein and flavor!

www.ingramcontent.com/pod-product-compliance
Lightning Source LLC
LaVergne TN
LVHW061943070526
838199LV00060B/3955